I Will Lift Up Mine Eyes

I Will Lift Up Mine Eyes

Inspiring Words
of Comfort and Hope

Selected by
Bette Bishop

Illustrated by
Paula Krekovich

HALLMARK EDITIONS

Foreword

There are moments, even in the happiest of lives, when we long to be comforted. Then we seek the warmth of consoling thoughts, of uplifting messages that give hope of a brighter tomorrow. *I Will Lift Up Mine Eyes* offers those messages in the eloquent writings of poets, philosophers, and religious leaders of all times: words of comfort, prayers of faith, voices of courage, songs of hope. It is a book that will encourage and inspire—and lift the heart.

The Beatitudes

Blessed are the poor in spirit: for theirs is the kingdom of heaven.

Blessed are they that mourn: for they shall be comforted.

Blessed are the meek: for they shall inherit the earth.

Blessed are they which do hunger and thirst after righteousness: for they shall be filled.

Blessed are the merciful: for they shall obtain mercy.

Blessed are the pure in heart: for they shall see God.

Blessed are the peacemakers: for they shall be called the children of God.

Blessed are they which are persecuted for righteousness' sake: for theirs is the kingdom of heaven.

MATTHEW 5: 3-10

Gift from the Sea

I am seeking perhaps what Socrates asked for in the prayer from the *Phaedrus* when he said, "May the outward and inward man be one." I would like to achieve a state of inner spiritual grace from which I could function and give as I was meant to in the eye of God.

Vague as this definition may be, I believe most people are aware of periods in their lives when they seem to be "in grace" and other periods when they feel "out of grace," even though they may use different words to describe these states. In the first happy condition, one seems to carry all one's tasks before one lightly, as if borne along on a great tide; and in the opposite state one can hardly tie a shoestring. It is true that a large part of life consists in learning a technique of tying the shoestring, whether one is in grace or not. But there are techniques of living too; there are even techniques in the search for grace. And techniques can be cultivated. I have learned by some experience, by many examples, and by the writings of countless others before me, also occupied in the search, that certain environments, certain modes of life, certain rules of conduct are more conducive to inner and outer harmony than others. There are, in fact, certain roads that one may follow. Simplification of life is one of them.

Simplification of outward life is not enough. It is merely the outside. But I am starting with the outside. I am looking at the outside of a shell, the outside of my life—the shell. The complete answer is not to be found on the outside, in an outward mode of living. This is only a technique, a road to grace.

ANNE MORROW LINDBERGH

God's Will

What we see here of this world is but an expression of God's will, so to speak—a beautiful earth and sky and sea—beautiful affections and sorrows, wonderful changes and developments of creation, suns rising, stars shining, birds singing, clouds and shadows changing and fading, people loving each other, smiling and crying, the multiplied phenomena of Nature, multiplied in fact and in fancy, in Art and Science, in every way that a man's intellect or education can be brought to bear. And who is to say that we are to ignore all this, or not value them and love them, because there is another unknown world yet to come? Why, that unknown future world is but a manifestation of God Almighty's will, and a development of Nature, neither more nor less than this in which we are, and an angel glorified or a sparrow on a gutter are

9

equally part of His creation. The light upon all the saints in Heaven is just as much and no more God's work, and the sun which shall shine tomorrow upon this infinitesimal speck of creation.

WILLIAM MAKEPEACE THACKERAY

The Art of Hope

The well-known maxim, "While there is life there is hope," has deeper meaning in reverse: "While there is hope there is life."

Hope comes first, life follows. Hope gives power to life. Hope rouses life to continue, to expand, to grow, to reach out, to go on.

Hope sees a light where there isn't any.

Hope lights candles in millions of despairing hearts.

Hope is the miracle medicine of the mind. It inspires the will to live. Hope is the physician's strongest ally.

Hope is man's shield and buckler against defeat. "Hope," wrote Alexander Pope, "springs eternal in the human breast." And as long as it does man will triumph and move forward.

Hope never sounds retreat. Hope keeps the banners flying.

Hope revives ideals, renews dreams, revitalizes visions.

Hope scales the peak, wrestles with the impossible, achieves the highest aim.

"The word which God has written on the brow of every man," wrote Victor Hugo, "is Hope." As long as man has hope no situation is hopeless.

WILFERD A. PETERSON

When the Sun Bursts Forth

When mists have hung low over the hills, and the day has been dark with intermittent showers, at length great clouds begin to hurry across the sky, the wind rises, and the rain comes pouring down; then we look out and exclaim: "Why, this is the clearing-up shower." And when the floods have spent themselves, the clouds part to let the blue sky tremble through them, and the west wind bears them away seaward, and, though they are yet black and threatening, we see their silver edges as they pass, and know that just behind them are singing birds and glittering dewdrops; and, lo! while yet we look, the sun bursts forth, and lights them up in the eastern heaven with the glory of the rainbow.

HENRY WARD BEECHER

Comfort for Every Sorrow

The best remedy for those who are afraid, lonely, or unhappy is to go outside, somewhere where they can be quite alone with the heavens, nature, and God. Because only then does one feel that all is as it should be and that God wishes to see people happy, amidst the simple beauty of nature. As long as this exists, and it certainly always will, I know that then there will always be comfort for every sorrow, whatever the circumstances may be.

ANNE FRANK

The One Source

All things come from one source, from that ruling Reason of the Universe, either under a primary impulse from it or by way of consequence. And therefore the gape of the lion's jaws and poison and all noxious things, such as thorns and mire, are but after results of the grand and the beautiful. Look not then on these as alien to that which thou doest reverence, but turn thy thoughts to the one source of all things.

MARCUS AURELIUS

13

The Hand of Faith

God speaks sometimes through our circumstances and guides us, closing doors as well as opening them.

He will let you know what you must do, and what you must be. He is waiting for you to touch Him. The hand of faith is enough.

PETER MARSHALL

Responsibility to Life

We must learn to reawaken and keep ourselves awake, not by mechanical aids but by an infinite expectation of the dawn, which does not forsake us in our soundest sleep. I know of no more encouraging fact than the unquestionable ability of man to elevate his life by a conscious endeavor. It is something to be able to paint a particular picture, or to carve a statue, and so to make a few objects beautiful, but it is more glorious to carve and paint the very atmosphere and medium through which we look, which morally we can do. To affect the quality of the day, that is the highest of arts. Every man is tasked to make his life, even in its details, worthy of the contemplation of his most elevated and critical hour.

HENRY DAVID THOREAU

All our progress is an unfolding, like the vege-
table bud. You have first an instinct, then an
opinion, then a knowledge, as the plant has root,
bud, and fruit. Trust the instinct to the end, though
you can render no reason.

RALPH WALDO EMERSON

Words to Live By

The spectrum of love has nine ingredients:
Patience: "Love suffereth long."
Kindness: "And is kind."
Generosity: "Love envieth not."
Humility: "Love vaunteth not itself,
    is not puffed up."
Courtesy: "Doth not behave itself unseemly."
Unselfishness: "Seeketh not her own."
Good Temper: "Is not easily provoked."
Guilelessness: "Thinketh no evil."
Sincerity: "Rejoiceth not in iniquity,
    but rejoiceth in truth."

Patience; kindness; generosity; humility; courtesy; unselfishness; good temper; guilelessness;
sincerity—these make up the supreme gift, the
stature of the perfect man. You will observe that
all are in relation to men, in relation to life, in
relation to the known today and the near tomorrow, and not to the unknown eternity. We hear

much of love of God; Christ spoke much of love of man. We make a great deal of peace with Heaven; Christ made much of peace on earth. Religion is not a strange or added thing, but the inspiration of the secular life, the breathing of an eternal spirit through the temporal world. The supreme thing, in short, is not a thing at all, but the giving of a further finish to the multitudinous words and acts which make up the sum of every common day.

HENRY DRUMMOND

Lincoln's Letter to a Mother

Dear Madam—

I have been shown in the files of the War Department a statement of the Adjutant General of Massachusetts, that you are the mother of five sons who have died gloriously on the field of battle.

I feel how weak and fruitless must be any words of mine which should attempt to beguile you from the grief of a loss so overwhelming. But I cannot refrain from tendering to you the consolation that may be found in the thanks of the Republic they died to save.

I pray that our Heavenly Father may assuage the anguish of your bereavement, and leave you only the cherished memory of the loved and lost, and

the solemn pride that must be yours, to have laid
so costly a sacrifice upon the altar of Freedom.

ABRAHAM LINCOLN

To Have Faith

We have the God-given ability to believe, to have
faith—in God, in ourselves, and in our fellowmen.
Christ has told us "according to your faith, be it
unto you." What a wonderful promise in those
words.

We have only to put our problems before Him
with a humble and faithful heart and to believe
with the simple faith of a little child, and we are
promised His guidance and help. If our problems
are big, then our prayers should be equally big!
And the minute we believe that He has answered
our prayers, they have been answered, perhaps not
as we wanted or expected, but answered never-
theless. And they are right answers, too.

NORMAN VINCENT PEALE

When you have shut your doors, and darkened
your room, remember never to say that you are
alone; for God is within and your genius is within,
and what need have they of light to see what you
are doing?

EPICTETUS

An Inner Exaltation

There is within each of us a modulation, an inner exaltation, which lifts us above the buffetings with which events assail us. Likewise, it lifts us above dependence upon the gifts of events for our joy. Hence, our dependence upon events is not absolute; it is qualified by our spiritual freedom. Therefore, when we speak of resignation it is not sadness to which we refer, but the triumph of our will-to-live over whatever happens to us. And to become ourselves, to be spiritually alive, we must have passed beyond this point of resignation.

ALBERT SCHWEITZER

Speaking of Man

I believe that the capacity to desire, to enjoy, and to be satisfied are in large measure as innate as the shape of one's nose; that there are people born to be hearty regardless of life's buffets, and others who are so constituted that they pass through the world zestless and ready for melancholy. William James said there are some who are born with an eternal bottle of champagne to their credit. I would add to this that there are others who enter life with a chloroform sponge under their noses. . . .

The good life cannot be put into any phrase, since,

to begin with, one must have an appetite for living. The healthy appetite is the *sine qua non* of a human striving, effort, and seeking; satisfaction is a goal subjectively defined for each man.

ABRAHAM MYERSON, M.D.

Beauty

Our Creator would never have made such lovely days and have given us the deep hearts to enjoy them, above and beyond all thought, unless we were meant to be immortal.

NATHANIEL HAWTHORNE

Love All God's Creation

Love all God's creation, both the whole and every grain of sand. Love every leaf, every ray of light. Love the animals, love the plants, love each separate thing. If thou love each thing thou wilt perceive the mystery of God in all; and when once thou perceive this, thou wilt thenceforward grow every day to a fuller understanding of it: until thou come at last to love the whole world with a love that will then be all-embracing and universal.

FEODOR DOSTOEVSKI

One Solitary Life

He was born in an obscure village, the child of a peasant woman. He grew up in still another village, where he worked in a carpenter shop until he was thirty. Then for three years he was an itinerant preacher. He never wrote a book. He never held an office. He never had a family or owned a house. He didn't go to college. He never visited a big city. He never traveled two hundred miles from the place where he was born.

He did none of the things one usually associates with greatness. He had no credentials but himself. He was only thirty-three when the tide of public opinion turned against him. His friends ran away. He was turned over to his enemies and went

through the mockery of a trial. He was nailed to a cross between two thieves. While he was dying, his executioners gambled for his clothing, the only property he had on earth. When he was dead, he was laid in a borrowed grave through the pity of a friend.

Nineteen centuries have come and gone, and to-day he is the central figure of the human race and the leader of mankind's progress. All the armies that ever marched, all the navies that ever sailed, all the parliaments that ever sat, all the kings that ever reigned, put together, have not affected the life of man on this earth as much as that *One Solitary Life*.

ANONYMOUS

Light Shining Out of Darkness

God moves in a mysterious way
  His wonders to perform;
He plants His footsteps in the sea,
  And rides upon the storm.

Deep in the unfathomable mines
  Of never-failing skill
He treasures up His bright designs,
  And works His sovereign will.

Blind unbelief is sure to err,
  And scan His work in vain;
God is His own interpreter,
  And He will make it plain.

WILLIAM COWPER

Memory

It is an exquisite and beautiful thing in our nature, that, when the heart is touched and softened by some tranquil happiness or affectionate feeling, the memory of the dead comes over it most powerfully and irresistibly. It would seem almost as though our better thoughts and sympathies were charms, in virtue of which the soul is enabled to hold some vague and mysterious intercourse with the spirits of those whom we loved in life.

CHARLES DICKENS

22

Man

What a piece of work is a man! how noble in reason! how infinite in faculty! in form and moving how express and admirable! in action how like an angel! in apprehension how like a god! the beauty of the world! the paragon of animals!

WILLIAM SHAKESPEARE

23

Eternal Life

Lord, make me an instrument of Thy peace!
Where there is hatred . . . let me sow love.
Where there is injury . . . pardon.
Where there is doubt . . . faith.
Where there is despair . . . hope.
Where there is darkness . . . light.
Where there is sadness . . . joy.
O Divine Master, grant that I may not so much
    seek
To be consoled . . . as to console,
To be understood . . . as to understand,
To be loved . . . as to love;
For it is in giving . . . that we receive;
It is in pardoning . . . that we are pardoned;
It is in dying . . . that we are born to eternal
    life.

ST. FRANCIS OF ASSISSI

The Lord Is My Shepherd

The Lord is my shepherd; I shall not want.

He maketh me to lie down in green pastures: he leadeth me beside the still waters.

He restoreth my soul: he leadeth me in the paths of righteousness for his name's sake.

Yea, though I walk through the valley of the shadow of death, I will fear no evil: for thou art with me; thy rod and thy staff they comfort me.

Thou preparest a table before me in the presence of mine enemies: thou anointest my head with oil; my cup runneth over.

Surely goodness and mercy shall follow me all the days of my life; and I will dwell in the house of the Lord for ever.

PSALM 23

The Promise of God

Thou hast invited me "to ask, to seek, to knock"— assuring me that if I ask, it shall be given unto me; If I seek, I shall find; if I knock, it shall be opened unto me.

Help me to believe that, O God. Give me the faith to ask knowing that I shall receive. Give me

the faith to seek, believing that I shall surely find.
Give me the faith and the persistence to knock,
knowing that it shall be indeed opened unto me.

Help me to live the Christian life in daring faith
and humble trust, that there may be worked out in
me, even in me, Thy righteousness and goodness.
With a sense of adventure, I make this prayer.

PETER MARSHALL

For Inspiration

The Prayers I make will then be sweet indeed,
  If Thou the spirit by which I pray;
  My unassisted heart is barren clay;
Which of its native self can nothing feed;
Of good and pious works Thou art the seed
    Which quickens where Thou say'st it may;
    Unless Thou show us Thine own
                true way,
No man can find it! Father, Thou must lead!
Do Thou, then, breathe those thoughts into
                my mind
    By which such virtue may in me be bred
    That in Thy holy footsteps I may tread:
The fetters of my tongue do Thou unbind,
    That I may have the power to sing of Thee
    And sound Thy praises everlastingly.

MICHELANGELO

Equality of God

Bring us, O Lord, at our last awakening, into the house and gate of heaven, to enter into that gate and dwell in that house where there shall be no darkness nor dazzling, but one equal light; no noise nor silence, but one equal music; no fears nor hopes, but one equal possession; no ends nor beginnings, but one equal eternity; in the habitations of Thy glory and dominion, world without end. Amen.

JOHN DONNE

I Will Lift Up Mine Eyes

I will lift up mine eyes unto the hills,
from whence cometh my help.

My help cometh from the Lord, which made heaven and earth.

He will not suffer thy foot to be moved: he that keepeth thee will not slumber....

The Lord shall preserve thee from all evil: he shall preserve thy soul.

The Lord shall preserve thy going out and thy coming in from this time forth, and even for evermore.

PSALM 121: 1-3, 5-8

My Hope and Refuge

In Thee, O Lord God, I place my whole hope and refuge; on Thee I rest all my tribulation and anguish; for I find all to be weak and inconstant, whatsoever I behold out of Thee. For many friends cannot profit, nor strong helpers assist, nor the books of the learned afford comfort, nor any place, however retired and lonely, give shelter, unless Thou Thyself dost assist, strengthen, console, instruct, and guard us. For all things that seem to belong to the attainment of peace and felicity, without Thee, are nothing, and do bring in truth no felicity at all. Thou therefore art the Foundation of all that is good; and to hope in Thee above all things is the strongest comfort of Thy servants. To Thee, therefore, do I lift up mine eyes; in Thee, my God, the Father of mercies, do I put my trust. Amen.

THOMAS A KEMPIS

Prayer at Morning

The day returns and brings us the petty round of irritating concerns and duties. Help us to play the man, help us to perform them with laughter and kind faces, let cheerfulness abound with industry. Give us to go blithely on our business all this day, bring us to our resting beds weary and content and undishonored, and grant us in the end the gift of sleep.

ROBERT LOUIS STEVENSON

Burn, then, little lamp; glimmer straight
                and clear—
Hush! a rustling wing stirs, methinks the air:
He for whom I wait, thus ever comes to me;
Strange Power! I trust Thy might;
          trust Thou my constancy.

EMILY BRONTE

Thou Sparest All

For the whole world before thee is as a little grain of the balance, yea, as a drop of the morning dew that falleth down upon the earth. But thou hast mercy upon all; for thou canst do all things, and winkest at the sins of men, because they should amend. For thou lovest all the things that are, and abhorrest nothing which thou hast made: for never wouldst thou have made anything, if thou hadst hated it. And how could anything have endured, if it had not been thy will? or been preserved, if not called by thee? But thou sparest all: for they are thine, O Lord, thou lover of souls.

THE APOCRYPHA

31

Light of Light

O God the Son, Light of Light, the most true and perfect Light, from whom this light of the sun and the day had their beginning: Thou that art the Light shining in darkness enlightening everyone that cometh into the world! expel from me all clouds of ignorance, and give me true understanding, that in Thee and by Thee I may know the Father: whom to know is to live, and to serve is to reign.

HENRY VAUGHAN

To Every Thing There Is a Season

To every thing there is a season, and a time to every purpose under the heaven:

A time to be born, and a time to die; a time to plant, and a time to pluck up that which is planted; A time to kill, and a time to heal; a time to break down, and a time to build up;

A time to weep, and a time to laugh; a time to mourn, and a time to dance; a time to cast away stones, and a time to gather stones together; a time to embrace, and a time to refrain from embracing;

A time to get, and a time to lose; a time to keep, and a time to cast away; a time to rend, and a time to sew; a time to keep silence, and a time to speak;

A time to love, and a time to hate; a time of war, and a time of peace.

ECCLESIASTES 3:1-8

Watch Thou, Dear Lord

Watch Thou, dear Lord, with those who wake, or watch, or weep tonight, and give Thine angels charge over those who sleep. Tend Thy sick ones, O Lord Christ. Rest Thy weary ones. Bless Thy dying ones. Soothe Thy suffering ones. Pity Thine afflicted ones. Shield Thy joyous ones. And all, for Thy Love's sake. Amen.

ST. AUGUSTINE

Be Not Afraid

Be not afraid of life. Believe that life *is* worth living, and your belief will help create the fact. The "scientific proof" that you are right may not be clear before the day of judgment (or some stage of being which that expression may serve to symbolize) is reached. But the faithful fighters of this hour, or the beings that then and there will represent them, may then turn to the faint-hearted, who here decline to go on, with words like those with which Henry IV greeted the tardy Crillon after a great victory had been gained: "Hang yourself, brave Crillon! we fought at Arques, and you were not there."

WILLIAM JAMES

To Face the Future

Thou knowest, Father, the things of which we are afraid—the terror by night, the arrow by day that takes us unawares and often finds us without a vital, ready faith.

Help us to remember, O Christ, that Thou art victorious . . . reigning over all; that in due time, in Thine own good time, Thou wilt work all things together for good to them that love Thee, who are called according to Thy purpose.

May we find our refuge in that regnant faith, and so face the future without fear. Give to us Thy peace, through Jesus Christ, our Lord.

PETER MARSHALL

I Trust

I trust, and nothing that happens disturbs my trust. I recognize the benificence of the power which we all worship as supreme—Order, Fate, the Great Spirit, Nature, God. I recognize this power in the sun that makes all things grow and keeps life afoot. I make a friend of this indefinable force, and straightway feel glad, brave, and ready for any lot heaven may decree for me. This is my religion of optimism.

Experiencing a great sorrow is like entering a cave.

We are overwhelmed by the darkness, the loneliness, the homesickness. Sad thoughts, like bats, flutter about us in the gloom. We feel that there is no escape from the prison house of pain. But God in His loving-kindness has set on the invisible wall the lamp of faith—whose beams shall guide us back to the sunlit world where work and friends and service await us.

HELEN KELLER

Courage from hearts and not from numbers grow.

JOHN DRYDEN

Trust Thyself

Trust thyself: every heart vibrates to that iron string. Accept the place the divine providence has found for you, the society of your contemporaries, the connection of events. Great men have always done so, and confided themselves childlike to the genius of their age, betraying their preception that the absolutely trustworthy was seated at their heart, working through their hands, predominating in all their being. And we are now men, and must accept in the highest mind the same transcendent destiny; and not minors and invalids in a protected corner, not cowards fleeing before a revolution, but guides, redeemers, and benefactors, obeying the Almighty effort and advancing on chaos and the dark.

RALPH WALDO EMERSON

Tell Him

The little sharp vexations
    And the briars that cut the feet,
Why not take all to the Helper
    Who has never failed us yet?
Tell Him about the heartache,
    And tell Him the longings too,
Tell Him the baffled purpose
    When we scarce know what to do.
Then, leaving all our weakness
    With the One divinely strong,
Forget that we bore the burden
    And carry away the song.

PHILLIP BROOKS

Christ Speaks to Us

Pluck up thy courage, faint heart; what though thou be fearful, sorry and weary, and standeth in great dread of most painful torments, be of good comfort; for I myself have vanquished the whole world, and yet felt I far more fear, sorrow, weariness, and much more inward anguish too, when I considered my most bitter, painful Passion to press so fast upon me. He that is strong-hearted may find a thousand glorious valiant martyrs whose example he may right joyously follow. But thou now, O timorous and weak, silly sheep, think it sufficient for thee only to walk after me, which am thy shepherd and governor, and so mistrust thyself and put thy trust in me. Take hold on the hem of my garment, therefore; from thence shalt thou perceive such strength and relief to proceed. . . .

ST. THOMAS MORE

The Joy of Heaven

Through God's unfailing grace, our sorrows become easier to bear. In His divine plan, our suffering can be sanctified. It can purify us, draw us closer to Him and make us stronger instruments in sanctifying the world. Christ Himself chose suffering as the divine means of saving mankind. We should pray, therefore, for the courage that can only come from Him who died for our sins. By looking at sorrow as a blessing in disguise, we shall regard it not as a sign of failure but as a small price to pay for the everlasting peace and joy of heaven.

JAMES KELLER

Eternal Life

The life of every brute and plant on earth
  Is by the quick beams of the sacred fires
  From its combining potencies drawn forth.
But the Supreme Beningnity inspires
  Directly your life, making it to love
  Itself, and kindling it to fresh desires.
For thee this argument may further prove
  Your resurrection, if the thought be weighed
  How human flesh was formed to breathe
   and move,
When the first parents both of them were made.

DANTE ALIGHIERI

For Whom the Bell Tolls

No man is an island, entire of itself; every man is
a piece of the continent, a part of the main; if a
clod be washed away by the sea, Europe is the
less, as well as if a promontory were, as well as if
a manor of thy friends or of thine own were; any
man's death diminishes me, because I am involved
in mankind; and therefore never send to know for
whom the bell tolls; it tolls for thee.

JOHN DONNE

A Divine Power

If you see a man unterrified in the midst of dangers, untouched by desires, happy in adversity, peaceful amid the storm, will you not say: A divine power has descended upon that man?

Just as the rays of the sun do indeed touch the earth, but still abide at the source from which they are sent; even so the great and hallowed soul does indeed associate with us, but still cleaves to its origin; on that source it depends, thither it turns its gaze and strives to go.

SENECA

Of Adversity

The virtue of prosperity is temperance; the virtue of adversity is fortitude, which in morals is the more heroical virtue. Prosperity is the blessing of the Old Testament; adversity is the blessing of the New, which carrieth the greater benediction, and the clearer revelation of God's favor. Yet even in the Old Testament, if you listen to David's harp, you shall hear as many hearse-like airs as carols; and the pencil of the Holy Ghost hath labored more in describing the afflictions of Job than the felicities of Solomon. Prosperity is not without many fears and distastes; and adversity is not without comforts and hopes. We see in needleworks and embroideries, it is more pleasing to have a lively work upon a sad and solemn ground, than to have a dark and melancholy work upon a lightsome ground: judge therefore of the pleasure of the heart by the pleasure of the eye. Certainly virtue is like precious odors, most fragrant when they are incensed or crushed; for prosperity doth best discover vice; but adversity doth best discover virtue.

SIR FRANCIS BACON

A Bulwark of Strength

One must hope that each of us might increase our capacity for greater humility, that we might become more mature and hence give more of ourselves, and, in a broad sense, love more effectively.

These are the virtues that are cardinal in every religion and hence are the centers of interest of the rabbi and the priest and the minister in each of his parishioners. I happen to be one of those physicians who believes that these virtues are the center of our focus. In advocating this necessity to learn to love more effectively, one is mindful of the fact that every religion has taught us that God is love—and that it is from Him that one can gain strength—so well verbalized by the Psalmist: "I lift up mine

eyes unto the hills from whence cometh my help."
It is my conviction that this belief can be a bulwark
of strength in the life of every one of us.

WILLIAM MENNINGER, M. D.

I find the great thing in this world is not so much
where we stand, as in what direction we are
moving.

OLIVER WENDELL HOLMES

Invocation

At the last, tenderly,
From the walls of the powerful,
    fortress'd house,
From the clasp of the knitted locks—
    from the keep of the well-closed doors,
Let me be wafted.
Let me glide noiselessly forth;
With the key of softness unlock the locks—
    with a whisper,
Set open the doors, O Soul!
Tenderly! be not impatient!
(Strong is your hold, O mortal flesh!
Strong is your hold, O love.)

WALT WHITMAN

Difficulty is a severe instructor, set over us by the Supreme guardian and legislator, who knows us better than we know ourselves, and loves us better too. He that wrestles with us strengthens our nerves and sharpens our skill. Our antagonist is our helper.

EDMUND BURKE

My Refuge

At the onset of fear and alarm, or when trouble and stress are at hand, I will bless Him with special thanksgiving and muse upon His power, and rely on His mercies always, and come thereby to know that in His hand lies the judgment of all living, and that all His words are truth.

From THE DEAD SEA SCRIPTURES

Hope

The tree of knowledge we in Eden proved;
The tree of life was thence to heaven removed;
Hope is the growth of earth, the only plant
Which either heaven or paradise could want.
Hell knows it not, to us alone confined,
And cordial only to the human mind. . . .

ANNE, COUNTESS OF WINCHILSEA

The Witness of Nature

In Cairo, I secured a few grains of wheat that had slumbered for more than thirty centuries in an Egyptian tomb. As I looked at them this thought came into my mind: If one of those grains had been planted on the banks of the Nile the year after it grew, and all its lineal descendants had been planted and replanted from that time until now, its progeny would today be sufficiently numerous to feed the teeming millions of the world. An unbroken chain of life connects the earliest grains of wheat with the grains that we sow and reap. There

is in the grain of wheat an invisible something which has power to discard the body that we see, and from earth and air fashion a new body so much like the old one that we cannot tell one from the other. If this invisible germ of life in the grain of wheat can thus pass unimpaired through three thousand resurrections, I shall not doubt that my soul has power to clothe itself with a body suited to its new existence, when this earthly frame has crumbled into dust.

WILLIAM JENNINGS BRYAN

Let Nothing Disturb Thee

Let nothing disturb thee;
Let nothing dismay thee;
All things pass:
God never changes.
Patience attains
All that it strives for.
He who has God
Finds he lacks nothing:
God alone suffices.

ST. TERESA

A Good-Night

Close now thine eyes and rest secure;
Thy soul is safe enough, thy body sure;
    He that loves thee, he that keeps
And guards thee, never slumbers, never sleeps.
The smiling conscience in a sleeping breast
    Has only peace, has only rest;
    The music and the mirth of kings
Are all but very discords, when she sings;
    Then close thine eyes and rest secure;
No sleep so sweet as thine, no rest so sure.

FRANCIS QUARLES

Wait On

To talk with God,
No breath is lost—
    Talk on!
To walk with God,
No strength is lost—
    Walk on!
To wait on God,
No time is lost—
    Wait on!

FROM THE HINDI

They Also Serve

When I consider how my light is spent
Ere half my days in this dark world and wide,
And that one talent which is death to hide
Lodged with me useless, though my soul more
  bent
To serve therewith my Maker, and present
My true account, lest he returning chide,
"Doth God exact day-labor, light denied?"
I fondly ask. But Patience, to prevent
That murmur, soon replies, "God doth not need
Either man's work or his own gifts. Who best
Bear his mild yoke, they serve him best. His state
Is kingly: thousands at his bidding speed,
And post o'er land and ocean without rest;
They also serve who only stand and wait."

JOHN MILTON

Wings

Be like the bird
That, pausing in her flight
Awhile on boughs too slight,
    Feels them give way
Beneath her and yet sings,
Knowing that she hath wings.

VICTOR HUGO

From *You Can't Go Home Again*

Something has spoken in the night . . .
And told me I shall die, I know not where.
Saying:
"To lose the earth you know, for greater
          knowing;
To lose the life you have, for greater life;
To leave the friends you loved, for greater
          loving;
To find a land more kind than home, more large
          than earth—
Whereon the pillars of this earth are
          founded,
Toward which the conscience of the world is
          tending—
A wind is rising, and the rivers flow."

THOMAS WOLFE

The Fountain

Into the sunshine,
    Full of the light,
Leaping and flashing
    Morning and night.
Into the moonlight,
    Whiter than snow,
Waving so flower-like
    When the winds blow;
Into the starlight
    Rushing in spray,
Happy at midnight
    Happy by day;
Ever in motion
    Blithesome and cheery,
Still climbing heavenward,
    Never aweary;
Glorious fountain,
    Let my heart be
Fresh, changeful, constant,
    Upward, like thee!

JAMES RUSSELL LOWELL

The Beautiful Promises of God

God hath not promised skies always blue,
Flower-strewn pathways all our lives through.
God hath not promised sun without rain,
Joy without sorrow, peace without pain.
God hath not promised we shall not know
Toil and temptation, trouble and woe.
He hath not told us we shall not bear
Many a burden, many a care.
But God hath promised strength for the day,
Rest for the laborer, light for the way,
Grace for the trials, help from above,
Unfailing sympathy, undying love.

AUTHOR UNKNOWN

Chartless

I never saw a moor,
I never saw the sea;
Yet know I how the heather looks,
And what a wave must be.
I never spoke with God,
Nor visited in heaven;
Yet certain am I of the spot
As if the chart were given.

EMILY DICKINSON

God's Grandeur

The world is charged with the grandeur of God.
It will flame out, like shining from shook foil;
It gathers to a greatness, like the ooze of oil
Crushed. Why do men then now not reck
    his rod?
Generations have trod, have trod, have trod;
And all is seared with trade; bleared,
                     smeared with toil;
And wears man's smudge and shares man's smell;
                 the soil
Is bare now, nor can foot feel, being shod.

And for all this, nature is never spent;
There lives the dearest freshness deep down
          things;
And though the last lights off the black West
          went
Oh, morning, at the brown brink eastward
          springs—
Because the Holy Ghost over the bent
World broods with warm breast and with ah!
          bright wings.

GERARD MANLEY HOPKINS

Faith

Sorrow knocked at the door,
Faith answered,
And found no one there.

I Wandered Lonely as a Cloud

I wandered lonely as a cloud
That floats on high o'er vales and hills,
When all at once I saw a crowd,
A host of golden daffodils;
Beside the lake, beneath the trees,
Fluttering and dancing in the breeze.
The waves beside them danced; but they
Out-did the sparkling waves in glee;
A poet could not but be gay,
In such a jocund company:
I gazed—and gazed—but little thought
What wealth the show to me had brought.
For oft, when on my couch I lie
In vacant or in pensive mood,
They flash upon that inward eye
Which is the bliss of solitude;
And then my heart with pleasure fills,
And dances with the daffodils.

WILLIAM WORDSWORTH

From *Thanatopsis*

So live, that when thy summons comes to join
The innumerable caravan, which moves
To that mysterious realm, where each shall take
His chamber in the silent halls of death,
Thou go not, like the quarry-slave at night,
Scourged to his dungeon, but, sustained and
    soothed
By an unfaltering trust, approach thy grave,
Like one who wraps the drapery of his couch
About him, and lies down to pleasant dreams.

WILLIAM CULLEN BRYANT

From *The Chambered Nautilus*

Build thee more stately mansions,
           oh, my soul,
As the swift seasons roll!
    Leave thy low-vaulted past!
    Let each new temple, nobler than the last,
    Shut thee from heaven
           with a dome more vast,
Till thou at length art free,
Leaving thine outgrown shell
           by life's unresting sea!

OLIVER WENDELL HOLMES

Contrasts

If all the skies were sunshine
    Our faces would be fain
To feel once more upon them
    The cooling plash of rain.
If all the world were music,
    Our hearts would often long
For one sweet strain of silence,
    To break the endless song.
If life were always merry,
    Our souls would seek relief,
And rest from weary laughter
    In the quiet arms of grief.

HENRY VAN DYKE

From *The Sleep*

He giveth his beloved sleep. Psalm 127:2
Of all the thoughts of God that are
Borne inward into souls afar,
Among the Psalmist's music deep,
Now tell me if there any is,
For gift or grace, surpassing this:
" He giveth his beloved—sleep"?

ELIZABETH BARRETT BROWNING

Begin the Day With God

Every morning lean thine arms awhile
Upon the window-sill of heaven
And gaze upon thy Lord,
Then, with the vision in thy heart,
Turn strong to meet thy day.

THOMAS BLAKE

All nature is but art, unknown to thee;
All chance, direction which thou canst not see;
All discord, harmony not understood;
All partial evil, universal good.

ALEXANDER POPE

Set at the Castle Press in Bembo, a Venetian face
first cut in 1495 for the printer Aldus Manutius Romanus
and named by him in honor of the humanist poet
(later Cardinal) Pietro Bembo.
Printed on Hallmark Eggshell Book paper.
Designed by Virginia Orchard.